**DATE D**

# SEA TURTLES
## ARE AWESOME

by Mirella S. Miller

www.12StoryLibrary.com

12-Story Library is an imprint of Bookstaves and Press Room Editions

Produced for 12-Story Library by Red Line Editorial

Photographs ©: Andrey Armyagov/Shutterstock Images, cover, 1; Richard Whitcombe/Shutterstock Images, 4, 19; Rich Carey/Shutterstock Images, 5, 12, 14, 15, 16, 17, 23, 24, 28; Stephanie Rousseau/Shutterstock Images, 6; Vladimir Wrangel/Shutterstock Images, 7; Maxim S Pometun/ Shutterstock Images, 8; David Evison/Shutterstock Images, 9; Nico Traut/Shutterstock Images, 10; glacex/iStock/Thinkstock, 11; idreamphoto/Shutterstock Images, 13, 29; Shane Myers Photography/ Shutterstock Images, 18, 21; Vlad61/Shutterstock Images, 20; JB Manning/Shutterstock Images, 22; Norm Diver/Shutterstock Images, 25; StacieStauffSmith Photos/Shutterstock Images, 26; mangojuicy/ Shutterstock Images, 27

**Library of Congress Cataloging-in-Publication Data**
Names: Miller, Mirella S., author.
Title: Sea turtles are awesome / by Mirella S. Miller.
Description: Mankato, MN : 12 Story Library, [2017] | Series: Animals are
  awesome | Audience: Grades 4 to 6. | Includes bibliographical references
  and index.
Identifiers: LCCN 2016047133 (print) | LCCN 2016053549 (ebook) | ISBN
  9781632354372 (hardcover : alk. paper) | ISBN 9781632355058 (pbk. : alk.
  paper) | ISBN 9781621435570 (hosted e-book)
Subjects: LCSH: Sea turtles--Juvenile literature. | Marine reptiles--Juvenile
  literature.
Classification: LCC QL666.C536 M55 2017 (print) | LCC QL666.C536 (ebook) |
  DDC 597.92/8--dc23
LC record available at https://lccn.loc.gov/2016047133

Printed in China
022017

Access free, up-to-date content on this topic plus a full digital version of this book. Scan the QR code on page 31 or use your school's login at 12StoryLibrary.com.

# Table of Contents

# Sea Turtles Are Ancient Creatures of the Sea

A sea turtle glides through the ocean water. It pokes its head above the surface for air. Then it dives back underwater looking for food. Sea turtles are reptiles. These giant creatures are cold-blooded. This means their body temperature matches their environment.

Other reptiles include snakes and lizards.

Scientists divide sea turtles into two families. Sea turtles with bony plates on their shells belong to one family. The second family of sea turtles does not have bony plates. The leatherback sea turtle is the only turtle in this family.

Sea turtles live in warm waters in oceans and seas across the world.

Sea turtles are among the oldest living creatures on Earth. They have been around since the time of the dinosaurs. Ancient sea turtles were much longer than even the tallest human. They had shells and lived in marshes. Very few sea turtle fossils have been found. Scientists have found some in South America.

Sea turtles spend most of their lives in the water.

Many sea turtle species today are endangered. Habitat loss, climate change, and poaching are a few of the threats sea turtles face. There are many organizations working to protect these animals. This helps ensure they will be around for many more years.

## 110 million

**Approximate number of years sea turtles have lived on Earth.**

- Sea turtles are reptiles.
- Sea turtles are cold-blooded.
- Sea turtles belong to one of two scientific families.
- Some sea turtle fossils have been found in South America.

## THINK ABOUT IT

Based on what you have read, what have scientists learned from sea turtle fossils?

# There Are Several Species of Sea Turtles

Seven species of sea turtles are found around the world. Sea turtles spend most of their time in the water. They have long life spans. Leatherbacks are the largest sea turtle species. They are also one of the largest reptiles. Adult males and females can grow to be longer than six feet (1.8 m). Leatherbacks are the only sea turtles without a hard shell. Leathery skin covers their backs.

Green sea turtles are the second-largest breed. They sometimes lie in the sun on beaches in Hawaii. Green sea turtles are endangered. Their shells are not usually green. They are named for their green body fat.

Leatherback turtles have hard, leathery skin instead of a shell.

# 30

**Average length, in inches (76 cm), of a Kemp's ridley sea turtle.**

- There are seven species of sea turtles.
- Leatherback sea turtles do not have hard shells.
- Olive ridley sea turtles are the most common species.
- The Kemp's ridley is the smallest species.

Loggerhead turtles have short front flippers.

Loggerheads are named for their large heads and strong jaws. They live in most of the world's oceans. But most female loggerheads make their nests in Florida.

Hawksbill sea turtles have colorful shells. They are sometimes seen swimming in coral reefs. Their sharp, narrow beaks help them reach food in reef cracks.

Flatback sea turtles are named for their flat shells. Very little is known about this species. They live in a small area of northern Australia.

Olive ridley sea turtles are the second-smallest species. They are named after their light-green coloring. Olive ridley turtles are the most common species of sea turtles. They are found around the world.

Kemp's ridley sea turtles are the smallest species. They have hooked beaks that help them eat crabs. Large groups of females nest together. Many of these turtles are found in the Gulf of Mexico.

# Sea Turtles Lay Their Eggs Ashore

Sea turtles spend most of their time alone in the ocean, but they begin their lives on land. When females become pregnant, they carry their eggs inside their bodies for 6 to 10 weeks. Then they return to the beaches where they were born to lay their eggs.

Every year, female sea turtles leave the water to nest on beaches. Most species nest alone. Others nest in large groups. Females spend a lot of time and energy building their nests. They need to keep their eggs safe from predators. Most sea turtles build their nests during the warm summer months, but leatherback turtles build them in the fall and winter.

A sea turtle in the Galapagos comes ashore to lay her eggs.

# 2

**Approximate number of hours it takes a female to build her nest.**

- Females spend a lot of time and energy building nests.
- Females come ashore to build nests and lay their eggs.
- Leatherback turtles lay their eggs in the fall and winter.
- Females use their flippers to dig the nests.
- Females lay between 50 and 200 eggs.

## NEST TEMPERATURE

The genders of hatchlings are determined by the temperature of their nests. A warmer nest produces more female sea turtles. A cooler temperature means there will be more males. If the temperature is moderate, there will be a mix of males and females.

Females leave the water at night. They move slowly on land. First, the female uses her flippers to dig a pit for her body. Then she digs a hole for her eggs. When she is done digging, the female lays her eggs. The eggs are soft and do not break when they fall into the pit. Females may lay between 50 and 200 eggs, depending on the species.

A green sea turtle lays her eggs on a beach at night.

9

# Sea Turtle Hatchlings Race to the Ocean

After laying all her eggs, the female sea turtle covers her nest with sand. She packs it down. This makes it harder for predators to find the eggs. Then the female returns to the ocean.

The eggs sit in the nest for approximately two months. Then the hatchlings make their way out of the eggs. It may take up to a week for the hatchlings to get to the surface of the sand. After all the eggs hatch, the hatchlings must get to the ocean.

Hatchlings travel in a pack across the sand to the ocean. They move

A female sea turtle covers the nest after laying eggs.

> Baby sea turtles get swept into the water when the tide comes in.

at night to avoid predators. Many of the hatchlings will not make it to adulthood because there are too many threats.

It takes approximately 10 to 50 years for sea turtles to reach adulthood, depending on the species. This is when they begin mating. Sea turtles leave the coastal waters and make their way to breeding areas. The only sea turtles that do not migrate are flatbacks. Female sea turtles mate once every two to three years. Kemp's ridley sea turtles are an exception. They mate yearly. Sea turtles can live up to 80 years.

## YOUNG SEA TURTLES

Young sea turtles spend up to 10 years hunting for food on their own. They swim where there is a lot of prey. During these years, sea turtles grow to be the size of a dinner plate. Scientists have a hard time tracking young sea turtles, since it is unclear where they rest or swim.

# 60
**Approximate number of days it takes for sea turtle eggs to incubate.**

- It takes 10 to 50 years for sea turtles to reach adulthood.
- Sea turtles can live up to 80 years.
- It takes up to a week for hatchlings to emerge from the nest.

# Sea Turtles Use Flippers to Swim

Sea turtles' bodies are built for swimming and moving easily through the water. Their bodies are large and powerful. Male and female turtles grow to be similar sizes. Sea turtles can dive to depths of 3,000 feet (914 m), and they can swim for miles at a time. Their shells and flippers help them do both of these things. Their smooth shells move easily through the water.

Most species of sea turtles have hard shells on their backs. They

Olive ridley sea turtles have heart-shaped shells.

are made up of bones. Some shells are oval shaped, but others look similar to a heart shape. Sea turtles' undersides are also covered in a shell. It is called a plastron. A sea turtle's shell helps protect its internal organs, but sea turtles cannot pull their heads and legs into their shells for protection.

A sea turtle's front flippers are long and skinny. These flippers help them dive deep into the water. Their back flippers are shorter. Flippers work similarly to boat paddles. The back flippers help steer the turtle through the water. Females also use their flippers to dig nests.

Sea turtles use their flippers to paddle through the water.

# Sea Turtles Have Sharp Senses and Camouflage

Like other reptiles, the sea turtle has a bone in its middle ear. This small bone makes vibrations for the inner ear. The sea turtle hears these vibrations and other low sounds, which are then picked up by its brain. This helps the sea turtle find food. It also keeps it safe from predators.

Sea turtles have great eyesight underwater. Multiple eyelids protect each eye. Sea turtles' eyes can see colors and shapes. They can also sense brightness. Sea turtles cannot see as well on land. Hatchlings use the moonlight to find their way to the ocean.

Scientists believe sea turtles can smell prey in the water. This is useful

Sea turtles have large upper eyelids.

# 4

**Number of eyelids sea turtles have.**

- A small bone makes vibrations in a sea turtle's ear.
- Sea turtles have great eyesight underwater.
- Sea turtles can smell prey in the water.
- Sea turtles have countershading.

## THINK ABOUT IT

Sea turtles use countershading to hide from predators. What other marine animals use this type of camouflage? Do a little research to find out.

for finding food when the water is not clear. They pull water in through their noses to smell.

The color of a sea turtle depends on the species. Sea turtles may be yellow, green, or black. Sea turtles have a type of camouflage called countershading. The tops of their shells are dark to match the ocean floor. Predators from above cannot see the sea turtles. The bottoms of their shells are light in color. This means marine animals looking skyward will not see the turtles either.

Sea turtles use their noses to smell underwater.

# Sea Turtles Eat Jellyfish and Seaweed

Sea turtles eat a variety of foods. Some species eat meat, but others eat only plants. Other sea turtles eat both meat and plants. Sea turtles do not have teeth. Instead, they have strong jaws. The jaws and beaks of each species are different. They are adapted for the diet of each species.

Green sea turtles have sharp beaks that are jagged like the edge of a knife. This helps them eat from seagrass beds. It also helps them scrape algae off rocks. Young green sea turtles eat meat, too. They hunt for worms and insects, along with plants.

Hawksbill sea turtles have narrow heads with sharp jaws. This helps them find food in small, tight places between rocks. They eat mostly sponges, shrimp, and squid.

Leatherbacks eat only soft foods. They do not have strong jaws to break hard shells. They eat mostly

A hawksbill sea turtle eats coral from a reef in the ocean.

A hawksbill turtle opens its mouth wide, showing it has no teeth.

jellyfish, seaweed, and fish. They can consume more than twice their body weight in one day.

Flatback sea turtles eat sea cucumbers, jellyfish, and seaweed.

## 1,200
**Weight, in pounds (544 kg), of sponges a hawksbill sea turtle eats in one year.**

- Green sea turtles eat algae and seagrasses.
- Leatherbacks eat twice their weight in one day.
- Flatbacks eat seaweed, sea cucumbers, and shrimp.
- Loggerheads, Kemp's ridleys, and olive ridleys use their strong jaws to crush and grind food.

They may also eat shrimp, crab, and fish.

Loggerheads, Kemp's ridleys, and olive ridleys have strong jaws. They are able to crush and grind food. These turtles eat crabs, shrimp, and jellyfish.

## HARMFUL SPONGES

Sponges are a hawksbill sea turtle's main food source. They are made up of tiny glass-like needles. But the needles do not seem to hurt the turtles. Some sponges are toxic. Hawksbills absorb the toxins into their body fat. Some humans illegally kill hawksbills for their meat. The toxins in the turtles' meat could kill humans.

17

# Sea Turtles Swim Alone in the Ocean

Sea turtles are not social animals. They spend most of their adult lives on their own in the ocean. Sea turtles will gather together during mating season. Some species, such as female olive ridley sea turtles, nest in groups on land. But for the most part, sea turtles spend their time alone.

Most sea turtles live alone, except for when they are mating.

Sea turtles spend a great deal of time underwater. They must come to the surface for air. Sea turtles are cold-blooded. This allows them to stay underwater longer. It also means sea turtles can dive deeper before coming up for air.

Flatback sea turtles float at the water's surface. They may do this for hours, resting or sunbathing. Sometimes birds will stand on the turtles' backs.

Green sea turtles and olive ridley sea turtles sometimes come ashore to sunbathe. It is common to see green sea turtles on beaches in Hawaii and the Galapagos Islands. Green sea turtles may sleep at the water's surface. Or they may sleep under rocks in shallow water.

When hawksbills rest, they hide. They have been found in coral reefs and between rocks. Scientists believe hawksbills sleep in the same spot each night.

# 5
**Number of hours green sea turtles can stay underwater before coming up for air.**

- Sea turtles mostly live alone.
- Flatbacks float at the water's surface for hours.
- Hawksbill sea turtles sleep in the same spot each night.
- Green sea turtles and olive ridleys sunbathe on the shore.

A hawksbill sea turtle hides under coral.

# Sea Turtles Live in Warm, Shallow Waters

Sea turtles live in warm and temperate ocean waters. They live all around the world. Adult sea turtles spend time in coastal waters and bays, but some may swim in deeper waters. Young sea turtles spend time in shallower waters.

Green sea turtles live in tropical waters near coasts and islands. This includes parts of the Atlantic Ocean and the Gulf of Mexico. Green sea turtles live in bays and other areas with seagrass beds. Loggerheads have a wider habitat range. They live in open waters worldwide, as well as bays, creeks, and coral reefs in shallower waters.

A green sea turtle swims in the warm waters of the Pacific Ocean around Hawaii.

Kemp's ridley sea turtles live only in the Gulf of Mexico. Their habitats have sandy or muddy seafloors where they can find lots of prey. Flatback sea turtles also live in only one part of the world. They are found on Australia's coasts.

## 160

**Maximum depth, in feet (49 m), where Kemp's ridley sea turtles swim.**

- Green sea turtles live in tropical waters near coasts and islands.
- Loggerheads are found worldwide in open water and shallow water.
- Kemp's ridley sea turtles live in the Gulf of Mexico.
- Leatherbacks have the widest habitat range.

Olive ridley sea turtles live in coastal tropical waters, including the Atlantic, Pacific, and Indian Oceans. Hawksbills are the most tropical of the sea turtle species. They are found near coral reefs and rocky areas.

Leatherbacks have the widest habitat range. They are found in the Pacific, Atlantic, and Indian Oceans. They live farther north than any other sea turtle species. They live mostly in open waters.

## THINK ABOUT IT

Why do you think sea turtles prefer to live in warm, shallow waters?

# Sea Turtles Migrate Each Year

Only female sea turtles come ashore. Young sea turtles and males do not. This makes it hard for scientists to track total sea turtle populations. Instead, scientists track the changing number of females nesting each year.

All sea turtle species migrate, but the distance they travel depends on the species. Sea turtles travel between nesting and feeding areas. They also travel to warmer waters, depending on the season. Scientists tag some sea turtles so they can track their migration.

Leatherback sea turtles travel the longest distances each year. They move in search of jellyfish. They swim across the entire Pacific Ocean, from Asia to the West Coast of the United States. Loggerheads also travel

A park ranger in Corpus Christi, Texas, monitors a Kemp's ridley sea turtle laying her eggs.

# 10,000

**Record distance, in miles (16,100 km), a leatherback travels in one year.**

- Scientists track the number of females nesting.
- All sea turtles migrate for food, nesting, or warmer waters.
- Leatherbacks swim across the entire Pacific Ocean.
- Little is known about hawksbill migration patterns.

## KNOWING WHEN TO MIGRATE

Leatherbacks have a special gland that may help them know when it is time to migrate. There is a small pink spot on the top of the leatherback's head. It is above the brain. Scientists believe this spot allows light to reach the pineal gland. This gland signals a change in season, letting the turtle know it is time to migrate.

Some sea turtles migrate thousands of miles each year.

thousands of miles. They swim between Japan and California.

Green sea turtles travel along coastlines. Some will venture farther to nest. Kemp's ridleys follow two main paths in the Gulf of Mexico. They swim north toward Mississippi or south toward Mexico. Flatbacks travel only a few hundred miles when they migrate. Unlike other species, olive ridleys travel in packs. Very little is known about hawksbill migration patterns.

# Sea Turtles Face Many Threats

Only a small percentage of sea turtle hatchlings make it to adulthood. There are many natural and human threats to hatchlings. Some animals, such as raccoons, ants, and crabs, wait for female sea turtles to finish laying their eggs. Then they feast on the eggs. Birds watch over beaches to grab up hatchlings. As turtles grow, there are fewer natural threats, but adult sea turtles still have predators. Some are attacked by sharks.

Sea turtles are common foods in some cultures. Some people eat both the meat and the eggs. The most commonly eaten species is the green sea turtle.

Garbage in the ocean is a threat to sea turtles.

Sea turtles can get tangled in fishing nets.

In some places, people use sea turtle shells for jewelry. Hawksbill shells are the most popular for this practice. Buying, selling, and importing turtle products is illegal in many countries. But many of the laws are not very strong, and people often ignore them.

Fishing is a big industry for many countries. Oceans around the world are filled with fishing nets. Turtles often get caught in these nets. They may be severely injured or even killed. Plastic and other debris in the water is also harmful. Sea turtles can get caught in it. Or they may eat garbage and become sick.

## 90

**Percentage the hawksbill sea turtle population has declined over the past 100 years.**

- Only a small percentage of hatchlings live to adulthood.
- Some humans kill sea turtles for their meat, eggs, or shells.
- Sea turtles can be injured or killed by fishing nets.

## LIGHTS

Female sea turtles choose to nest on dark beaches. Hatchlings use the moonlight to guide them to the ocean. If bright artificial lights are shining, they can confuse hatchlings. The hatchlings may move toward the light instead of the water. Some coastal communities turn their lights off at night so hatchlings are not confused.

25

# Saving the Sea Turtles

Nearly all sea turtle species are endangered. They are legally protected by governments, but they are still in danger of becoming extinct. In the United States, it is illegal to harm or kill sea turtles, their eggs, or their hatchlings. It is also illegal to import or sell turtle products. Some states have specific laws focused on turtle habitats.

Internationally, sea turtles are protected from trade by countries that have signed a treaty. But countries around the world must do much more to help sea turtles survive. Feeding and nesting

In South Carolina, signs posted in nesting areas warn people of the laws protecting sea turtles.

**LOGGERHEAD TURTLE NESTING AREA**

Eggs, Hatchlings, Adults, and Carcasses are Protected By Federal & State Laws

Contact
1-800-922-5431
www.dnr.sc.gov/seaturtle/

grounds need to be protected from human threats.

Humans can help. Researchers monitor nesting beaches. They place screens over turtle nests. This keeps eggs safe from predators. Researchers sometimes move the eggs to a safer location. Scientists are trying to reduce artificial lights on beaches. This leads to less confusion for hatchlings. It helps ensure they make it to the ocean, where they have a better chance of survival.

Visitors to beaches can help pick up trash. They can also stay away from sea turtles and their nests. This gives turtles space to thrive in their habitat.

# 30 million

**Approximate number of eggs olive ridley sea turtles lay on one beach in Costa Rica each year.**

- Sea turtles are legally protected but still in danger.
- The United States has laws protecting sea turtles.
- Countries around the world need to work together to protect sea turtles.
- Researchers help keep nests safe from predators.

Sometimes, researchers put protective barriers around the places where sea turtles lay their eggs.

# Fact Sheet

- Sea turtles are threatened by human activities. Oil spills, pollution, climate change, and beach erosion are threats to sea turtle populations.

- After a female lays her eggs, she camouflages the nest. She covers it with a mix of dry and wet sand before she goes back to the ocean. She never returns to her eggs. A female may lay eggs a few times each nesting season.

- Females nest on the same beach where they were born. Scientists do not know why. One theory is that sea turtles can sense Earth's magnetic fields. This allows them to find their way back to a certain beach.

- The largest sea turtles lived during the time of the dinosaurs. They were called *Archelon*. They grew to be approximately 21 feet (6.4 m) in length.

- The Pacific leatherback is the fastest aquatic reptile. It can swim at speeds up to 22 miles per hour (35 km/h).

- Sea turtles have a salt gland to get rid of extra salt. Other marine animals have this, too. The gland empties the salt through the sea turtles' eyes. It makes it look as if the turtles are crying. The tears help keep sand out of the females' eyes while they dig their nests.

- Singer Island in Florida is an important beach for sea turtle nesting. Loggerheads, green sea turtles, and leatherbacks build their nests on this beach every year. Organizations protect this area to ensure it continues to be a safe habitat for sea turtles.

# Glossary

**camouflage**
A protective coloration in animals that helps them blend in with their environments.

**climate change**
Changes in weather patterns on Earth.

**countershading**
Coloration on an animal that makes it difficult for predators to see the animal.

**endangered**
An animal that is threatened with extinction.

**fossils**
The remains of plants or animals that are preserved in earth or rock.

**hatchlings**
Young animals that have just come out of their eggs.

**poaching**
To hunt illegally.

**predators**
Animals that live by hunting, killing, and eating other animals.

**prey**
An animal that is hunted by other animals for food.

**species**
A group of animals that is similar.

**toxic**
Having poisonous substances.

**vibrations**
Slight continuous shaking motions.

# For More Information

## Books

Einspruch, Andrew. *Migration: Animals on the Move.* New York: PowerKids, 2015.

Hirsch, Rebecca. *Green Sea Turtles: A Nesting Journey.* Minneapolis, MN: AV2 by Weigl, 2017.

Schuetz, Kari. *Sea Turtles.* Minneapolis, MN: Bellwether, 2017.

## Visit 12StoryLibrary.com

Scan the code or use your school's login at **12StoryLibrary.com** for recent updates about this topic and a full digital version of this book. Enjoy free access to:

- Digital ebook
- Breaking news updates
- Live content feeds
- Videos, interactive maps, and graphics
- Additional web resources

**Note to educators:** Visit 12StoryLibrary.com/register to sign up for free premium website access. Enjoy live content plus a full digital version of every 12-Story Library book you own for every student at your school.

31

# Index

## About the Author

Mirella S. Miller is an author and editor of several children's books. She lives in Minnesota with her husband and dogs.